The Essential B

MERCEDE
190

All 190 models (W201 series) 1982 to 1993

Your marque expert:
Julian Parish

VELOCE PUBLISHING
THE PUBLISHER OF FINE AUTOMOTIVE BOOKS

www.veloce.co.uk

First published in March 2018 by Veloce Publishing Limited, Veloce House, Parkway Farm Business Park, Middle Farm Way,
Poundbury, Dorchester, Dorset, DT1 3AR, England.
Telephone 01305 260068/Fax 01305 250479/e-mail info@veloce.co.uk/web www.veloce.co.uk or www.velocebooks.com.
ISBN: 978-1-845849-27-6 UPC: 6-36847-04927-0

British Library Cataloguing in Publication Data – A catalogue record for this book is available from the British Library.
Typesetting, design and page make-up all by Veloce Publishing Ltd on Apple Mac.
Printed and bound in India by Replika Press.

Introduction
– the purpose of this book

Today, we take the Mercedes C-Class for granted as one of its manufacturer's most successful models. But it is with the 190 range, launched in November 1982, that the origins of Mercedes' compact executive model lie. Codenamed W201, but nicknamed the 'Baby Benz,' the 190 marked Mercedes-Benz' return to a much smaller class of car than it had produced for many years. The energy crisis of 1973 and the success of BMW's smaller 02 and 3-Series models prompted Mercedes' management to focus on a new and more efficient generation of cars, and development of the 190 began in 1977.

Designed by Bruno Sacco, the styling of the 190 was a major break with tradition, and its square-cut, modern lines set the tone for the R129 SL and W124 models which followed. Its body had a low drag coefficient (Cd) of just 0.33, helping to reduce fuel consumption and meet the Corporate Average Fuel Economy (CAFE) requirements in the US. Mercedes was keen to retain a high standard of refinement in its smallest model, and the 190 had sophisticated, multi-link rear suspension. As with the earlier W123, safety was a major consideration, and the 190 featured a deformable crash cell and specially designed door locks; seatbelt tensioners became standard in 1984, while ABS and a driver's airbag were also available.

**The pre-face-lift 190 range, with the 2.3-16 in the foreground.
(Courtesy Mercedes-Benz Classic)**

Efficient and unassuming the 190 may have been, but there was another side to its character. Alongside the mainstream petrol and diesel-engined saloons, in 1984 Mercedes introduced the 2.3-16: an unashamedly sporty model, with a Cosworth-designed 16-valve cylinder head, uprated suspension, and even a bodykit! The motorsport versions of the 190 enjoyed huge success in the DTM touring car championship, while the 2.3-16 established 12 international endurance records at the Nardo test track.

Efficient shape of the 190 developed in the wind tunnel. (Courtesy Mercedes-Benz Classic)

The 190 is sometimes overlooked by prospective owners of modern classics, who favour the more traditional appearance of Mercedes' W123, or the wider range of body styles of the W124. Whether as a first-time modern classic or for everyday use, however, it makes a strong case for itself. The 190 was extremely well built and, when newer, consistently achieved excellent results in the German TÜV safety inspection. Today, it remains generally reliable, with few electronic components to go wrong. The 190 rusts less than many cars of its age – less, in fact, than the W202 C-Class which succeeded it. The 2.3-16 and 2.5-16 models, meanwhile, have already attained cult status among lovers of performance saloons of the 1980s and '90s.

Interior of a 190E saloon with manual transmission. (Courtesy Mercedes-Benz Classic)

Thanks

I am grateful to Mark Taylor of MTSV, one of the first specialists in the UK to concentrate on the 190, and to Dave Richards at Project Shop and Sascha Siebertz at AixClusive Cars for sharing their knowledge and experience. Rory Lumsdon and Rachel Goodwin at Mercedes-Benz UK, and Silvie Kiefer at Mercedes-Benz Classic in Stuttgart provided valuable access to information and archive images.

Finally, it is my pleasure to thank once again Rod Grainger, Lizzie Bennett and the team at Veloce Publishing.

Contents

1 Is it the right car for you?

– marriage guidance

Tall and short drivers

Most drivers should be comfortable behind the wheel, although some larger drivers may find that the large (non-adjustable) steering wheel makes getting in and out harder.

Weight of controls

A few early cars (in 1983/84) were not fitted with power steering, which will make the car heavy to drive. The other controls feel solid and well-weighted.

Will it fit the garage?

Model	Length	Width	Height
190D/E until 1988	174.0in/4420mm	66.1in/1678mm	54.7in/1390mm
190D/E from 1988	175.1in/4448mm	66.5in/1690mm	54.7in/1390mm
190E 2.3-16/2.5-16	174.4in/4430mm	67.2in/1706mm	53.6in/1361mm

Interior space

The doors open wide, giving good access for passengers. Space in the front is fine, although the 190 may seem narrow in comparison with newer cars. Legroom in the rear is relatively cramped, albeit slightly better on post-face-lift cars thanks to a revised seat design. The 16-valve versions and some cars with the optional Sportline trim had individual bucket-style seats in the back.

Luggage capacity

The boot (trunk) is reasonably sized for a car of this type, with a capacity of 14.5ft^3 (410l). The rear seat backrest does not fold, however, and luggage must be loaded over a high lip.

Usability

Many 190s have remained in daily use ever since they were new. Their solid construction and ease of driving make them ideal as first-time modern classics.

Parts availability

Most mechanical and service parts remain available. Where Mercedes-Benz itself can no longer supply parts, owners' clubs and independent specialists can often step in. Plenty of cars are being scrapped and are a further source of parts. Some interior trim, however, can be difficult to find, particularly in less common colours. Parts which are specific to the 16-valve models, such as

Sober but elegant lines of a post-face-lift 190E saloon. (Courtesy Mercedes-Benz Classic)

the extra instruments in the centre console, can also be harder to track down. This is even more the case with parts unique to the rare Evo/Evo II and AMG models.

Service costs
Most routine service parts and consumables are reasonably priced. Some parts which have gone out of stock are now being remanufactured, but at higher prices than before. The 190 is generally a straightforward car to work on for the home mechanic or professional workshop, helping to keep maintenance costs down.

Insurance
Most insurers will now cover the 190 under classic car policies, sometimes with mileage limitations or alongside a modern 'daily driver.'

Investment potential
Prices of the Evo and Evo II models have already skyrocketed, with those of the AMG 3.2 also climbing. The 'ordinary' 16-valve versions are now sought-after performance saloons, and values are continuing to move up. Good 190E 2.6 models are becoming scarce, and prices are starting to rise. Values of other 190/190E and 190D versions are stable or increasing only slightly.

Foibles
It is hard to think of a car with fewer idiosyncrasies than the 190. Even the parking brake, that bugbear of many owners of Mercedes with manual transmission, is a conventional pull-up lever. On 16-valve models, first gear is down and to the left, but owners soon get used to this 'dogleg' layout.

Make sure the rear seats are roomy enough for your requirements. (Courtesy Mercedes-Benz Classic)

Plus points
• Excellent build quality and reliability
• Refined and comfortable, especially 190E 2.6
• 16-valve versions: strong performance

Minus points
• Diesel models (except 2.5 Turbo) slow by modern standards
• Mainstream models (190/190E and 190D) may be too plain for some
• Only available as a four-door saloon

Alternatives
Audi 80/90, BMW 3-Series, Saab 900, Ford Sierra Cosworth.

2.3-16 and later 2.5-16 models are increasingly in demand. (Courtesy Mercedes-Benz Classic)

2 Cost considerations
– affordable, or a money pit?

Purchase price
Prices vary hugely by model. A decent 190E, with under 100,000 miles recorded and a service history, can be found from ●x3000 to ●x7000. The 2.6-litre models fetch up to ●x10,000, with the highest prices reserved for the 190E 2.3-16 and 2.5-16 versions, which can command as much as ●x25,000. Evo and Evo II prices are off the dial: the auction record for the Evo II is nearly ●x270,000!

Servicing
A Mercedes 190 is a pretty straightforward car to look after, with a huge amount of information available online to help the home mechanic (see Chapter 16). Most service items are readily available and not too expensive.
• Oil and filter change: every year or 6000 miles
• Brake fluid: change every two years
• Sparkplugs: change every two years or 12,000 miles
• Coolant: change every three years
• Fuel and air filters: change every three years or 36,000 miles
• Simplex timing chain: change every 60,000 miles

Parts prices
Prices shown are for a post-face-lift 190E 2.0 saloon and are for OEM parts from Mercedes-Benz, unless noted otherwise. Many independents offer parts for the 190, but these can vary in quality. You may also find used parts from the many cars now being scrapped, which will be much cheaper.

190E saloon (blue) next to range-topping 190E 2.5-16.
(Courtesy Mercedes-Benz Classic)

Mechanical parts
Fuel filter ●x35
Distributor ●x90
Sparkplugs (set of 4) ●x10
Radiator ●x225
Coolant expansion tank ●x40
Cylinder head gasket ●x20
Timing chain kit (single-row) ●x180
Water pump ●x200
Exhaust manifold ●x550
Exhaust (complete) ●x510
Clutch kit ●x290
Driveshaft boot ●x10 (independent)
Front suspension: lower ball joint ●x20
Front shock absorber (each) ●x170
Rear shock absorber (each) ●x140
Rear spring (each) ●x90
Tyre: 185/65 R15 ●x60 (independent)
Front brake pads ●x20
Front brake discs (pair) ●x50
Rear brake pads ●x15
Rear brake discs (pair) ●x80
Battery ●x90

Body parts
Bonnet ●x320
Underbonnet insulation ●x15
Front wing ●x640
Rear wing ●x680
Front bumper ●x250
Rear bumper ●x260
Front door ●x530
Door seals (each) ●x180
Windscreen ●x300
Windscreen seal ●x50
Alloy wheel (15in) ●x100 (independent)
Halogen headlamp ●x280
Tail light assembly ●x140
Set of overmats ●x140 (independent)
Front seat cover (MB-Tex) ●x100

Exploded view of the 2.3-16's engine components.
(Courtesy Mercedes-Benz Classic)

190D, with its encapsulated diesel engine laid out
beside it. (Courtesy Mercedes-Benz Classic)

Driveshaft boot: an
inexpensive replacement.

3 Living with a 190

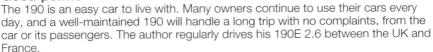

– will you get along together?

Good points

The 190 is an easy car to live with. Many owners continue to use their cars every day, and a well-maintained 190 will handle a long trip with no complaints, from the car or its passengers. The author regularly drives his 190E 2.6 between the UK and France.

The 190's design has aged well, and, even at 30 years old, the regular versions have an unpretentious appearance which appeals to many onlookers. By modern standards, the body feels quite compact and rather narrow, but that makes it easier to thread through gaps in traffic or park in tight spaces, helped by its excellent turning circle.

The 190 is comfortable, too, with firm but supportive seats and a superb chassis for its time, which offers a fine balance between ride comfort and roadholding. The Sportline chassis option further improves the 190's road manners, while the 2.3-16 and 2.5-16 versions are true enthusiasts' cars, with sharp handling and strong performance from their 16-valve engines.

For many years, Mercedes was renowned for building the best automatic transmissions in the business, and the 190 will not disappoint, with smooth – albeit not particularly fast – changes between its four ratios. It is generally a reliable box, to boot. Equipped with automatic transmission, and especially in six-cylinder 2.6-litre form, the 190's refinement belies its compact dimensions.

When buying a car 35 years after it was introduced, however, understated good looks and smooth driving alone are not enough. This is where the 190 can show its trump card: well designed and superbly built, its durability and reliability have become legendary, even by Mercedes' high standards in the 1980s. A study carried out by the German ADAC organisation, in 2001, showed the 190 to have the fewest breakdowns of any Mercedes model on record. Running costs, too, are very reasonable. If you appreciate high-quality German engineering and are reluctant to take on an older car which needs constant fettling, the 190 makes a great introduction to the pleasures of driving a future classic.

190 in its purest form: before the mid-life face-lift and with plastic wheel trims. (Courtesy Mercedes-Benz Classic)

Comfortable front seats, rational control layout and superb finish. (Courtesy MTSV)

The skirts and spoilers on this 2.5-16 won't appeal to everyone.
(Courtesy Mercedes-Benz Classic)

Bad points

Setting aside the 16-valve versions, the 190 is a car to buy with your head rather than your heart. For some enthusiasts, its looks may be just a little too plain and unassuming. Those owners who appreciate its straightforward appearance, on the other hand, may take exception to the bodykits fitted to the 16-valve versions, which Mercedes' traditional customers considered very infra dig when these versions were launched.

Performance varies hugely by model: while owners of the 16-valve and 2.6-litre versions should have few complaints, the diesel versions – with the exception of the 2.5 Turbo – are dismally slow by 21st century standards. Among the petrol-engined models, the original carburettor-fed 190 and later 190E 1.8 models are best described as merely adequate, but the 2-litre 190E versions offer an acceptable balance between modern performance and economy. The manual gearbox is long-lived, but has a notchy change. The 16-valve versions are true performance models, but their engines are less refined than you would expect from a conventional Mercedes saloon.

The trade-off for the Baby Benz' compact exterior dimensions is its interior space, with room in the back, in particular, quite limited. If you need more space for rear seat passengers, the larger, but similarly styled W124 model – also available

with a wide range of petrol and diesel engines – may be a better bet. The W124 also offers an estate option, if you need increased luggage capacity; the 190's rear seat is fixed, making it impossible to carry longer loads.

High lip and fixed rear seat limit the 190's load-carrying ability.
(Courtesy Mercedes-Benz UK)

4 Relative values
– which model for you?

The engine defines the personality of the 190, and choosing the right engine is key to picking the car to suit your driving style ... and your budget.

Throughout its career, the W201 was only produced as a four-door saloon with a separate boot (trunk). An attractive two-door convertible was prototyped, but never reached production.

The 190 was built before Mercedes introduced the myriad trim levels of later models: the 16-valve models have distinctive interior and exterior fittings, but otherwise the equipment fitted to each car really depends on the option boxes which its first owner checked, and, to some extent, its year of manufacture. Towards the end of production, a small number of limited-edition models were offered.

Which engine?

Originally billed 'The whispering diesel,' all the 190 diesels are relatively refined for their time, thanks to their encapsulated engines and extra sound-deadening. Introduced in North America in 1986 and in Europe the following year, the 2.5 Turbo, with a five-cylinder engine producing 122bhp, is the most pleasant to drive. The basic 2-litre 190D, however, could muster only 72bhp, and performance is sluggish. If you drive regularly in a city where the use of older cars with higher emissions may be restricted, think hard before buying any 190 diesel.

At its launch in 1982, the 190 came with a four-cylinder, two-litre petrol engine, in 90bhp carburettor or 122bhp fuel-injected form. A 2.3-litre fuel-injected 'four' was soon added to the range in North America and continental Europe, eventually producing 136bhp. From May 1990 until the end of production, the base 190 was replaced by a 1.8-litre fuel-injected model developing 109bhp, which was smoother and more refined.

If you are looking for outstanding mechanical refinement, however, the 190E 2.6, introduced in 1986, is the model to choose. Its straight-six engine offers decent performance and turbine-like smoothness throughout the rev range.

The 2.3-16 and 2.5-16 models can be recognised by their extended side skirts and front and rear spoilers, which reduced lift and improved high-speed stability.

Often referred to in the UK as the Cosworth Mercedes, the 2.3-16 was developed with motorsport in mind. Developing 185bhp, it had a Cosworth-designed 16-valve twin-cam head. The manual gearbox – a five-speed Getrag unit –

Pre-face-lift range, from base 190 to 2.3-16. (Courtesy Mercedes-Benz Classic)

The 2.5D Turbo can be recognised by this additional grille in the right-hand front wing. (Courtesy Mercedes-Benz Classic)

Sports seats, dogleg gearchange and extra instruments: it can only be a 16-valve model. (Courtesy Mercedes-Benz Classic)

Original brochure image for the exclusive AMG 3.2. (Courtesy Mercedes-Benz Classic)

was also new. The 2.3-16 was available only in smoke silver or blue-black metallic, while the new interior – with additional instruments and four individual sports seats – was available in black leather or part-leather and cloth.

In summer 1988, the 2.3-16 was replaced by the 2.5-16, although this was never officially sold in the US. Its engine, developed in-house by Mercedes and now producing 204bhp, was torquier and more flexible. Astral silver and almandine red were added to the range of colours. The 2.5-16 served as the basis for the bewinged Evo and Evo II homologation specials.

From 1983, AMG offered a tuned 2.3-litre four-cylinder version of the 190, but the most sought-after AMG model is the 3.2: fewer than 200 were built from 1990-93, with an enlarged M103 six-cylinder engine developing 234bhp and stiffer suspension.

Which transmission?

Mercedes' smooth and refined four-speed automatic – with a choice of standard and economy modes for the first time – seems a natural partner for the 190E 2.6, and also suits the torquey nature of the 190D 2.5 Turbo. The five-speed manual, on the other hand, is the choice of many enthusiasts for the 16-valve models. On the other models, the five-speed manual gearbox (standard on the 2.3 and 2.6, optional on other versions) provides the highest gearing for more relaxed cruising.

Which generation?

Despite its long career, the W201 range only went through one major face-lift, in August 1988: the post-face-lift cars can be identified by their side cladding panels, available in 12 different colours. The front and rear aprons were re-styled, while inside there was a new design for the cloth trim, improved rear seat space and extra equipment.

A final refresh followed in 1991, with body-coloured exterior mirrors and a full-length centre console finished in Zebrano wood, while, by 1992, ABS and a driver's airbag became standard on all models.

Post-face-lift car with revised front bumper and lower side panels.
(Courtesy Mercedes-Benz UK)

Special editions and trim

To reinforce the 190's sporting appeal, in 1989 Mercedes introduced the Sportline package in Europe: available with all engines, power was unchanged, but handling was improved with Bilstein shock absorbers and wider tyres on standard-fit alloy wheels. Individual bucket seats all round and check cloth trim were also available. In the US, the Sportline option was offered only on the 2.6 model, in 1992-93.

Towards the end of the 190's life in 1993, a special LE (Limited Edition) model was offered in the UK and Ireland, with 1.8- and 2-litre petrol engines, and extensive additional equipment including a Blaupunkt stereo, electric windows and sunroof, and burr walnut trim.

Full-length Zebrano wood centre console lifts the appearance of final models.
(Courtesy Mercedes-Benz UK)

Run-out Limited Edition model in UK, with LE badging.
(Courtesy MTSV)

5 Before you view
– be well informed

To avoid a wasted journey, and the disappointment of finding that the car does not match your expectations, it will help if you're very clear about what questions you want to ask before you pick up the telephone. Some of these points might appear basic, but when you're excited about the prospect of buying your dream classic, it's amazing how some of the most obvious things slip the mind … You can also check the current values of the model which attracts you in classic car magazines, which give both a price guide and auction results.

Where is the car?
Is it going to be worth travelling to the next county/state, or even across a border? A locally advertised car, although it may not sound very interesting, can add to your knowledge for very little effort, so make a visit – it might even be in better condition than expected.

Dealer or private sale
Establish early on if the car is being sold by its owner or by a trader. A private owner should have all the history, so don't be afraid to ask detailed questions. A dealer may have more limited knowledge of a car's history, but should have some documentation. A dealer may offer a warranty/guarantee (ask for a printed copy) and finance.

Cost of collection and delivery
A dealer may well be used to quoting for delivery by car transporter. A private owner may agree to meet you halfway, but only agree to this after you have seen the car at the vendor's address to validate the documents. Alternatively, you could meet halfway and agree the sale, but insist on meeting at the vendor's address for the handover.

View – when and where
It is always preferable to view at the vendor's home or business premises. In the case of a private sale, the car's documentation should tally with the vendor's name and address. Arrange to view only in daylight, and avoid a wet day. Most cars look better in poor light, or when wet.

Reason for sale
Do make it one of the first questions. Why is the car being sold, and how long has it been with the current owner? How many previous owners?

Imports
The 190 is a popular classic in Germany, with plenty on sale. Some German-market cars, especially from the lower end of the range, however, have a very basic specification.

When you buy a car from another country, you may need to make changes to the number (license) plates, lighting (headlamps and indicators) and radio equipment. If you re-register a car from Germany or another EU country within the

A special temporary registration is required to export a car from Germany.

EU, you may need to obtain an attestation from Mercedes-Benz that it conforms to the original specification.

Condition (body/chassis/interior/mechanicals)
Query the car's condition in as specific terms as possible – preferably citing the checklist items described in Chapter 9.

All original specification
An original equipment car is invariably of higher value than a customised version.

Matching data/legal ownership
Do Vehicle Identification Number (VIN)/chassis, engine numbers and licence plate match the official registration document? Is the owner's name and address recorded in the official registration documents?

Compare the VIN on the paperwork with the number stamped on the VIN plate on the car.

For those countries that require an annual test of roadworthiness, does the car have a document showing it complies (an MoT certificate in the UK, which can be verified on 0300 123 9000 or www.gov.uk/check-mot-status)?

If a smog/emissions certificate is mandatory, does the car have one?

If required, does the car carry a current road fund licence/licence plate tag?

Does the vendor own the car outright? Money might be owed to a finance company or bank: the car could even be stolen. Several organisations will supply the data on ownership, based on the car's licence plate number, for a fee. Such companies can often also tell you whether the car has been 'written-off' by an insurance company. In the UK, these organisations can supply vehicle data:

HPI – 0845 300 8905; hpi.co.uk
AA – 0800 316 3564; theaa.com
DVLA – 0300 790 6802; www.gov.uk/get-vehicle-information-from-dvla/
RAC – 0330 159 0364; www.rac.co.uk/

Other countries will have similar organisations.

Insurance
Check with your existing insurer before setting out, your current policy might not cover you to drive the car if you do purchase it.

How you can pay
A cheque (check) will take several days to clear and the seller may prefer to sell to a cash buyer. However, a banker's draft (a cheque issued by a bank) is as good as cash, but safer, so contact your own bank and become familiar with the formalities that are necessary to obtain one.

Buying at auction?
If the intention is to buy at auction, see Chapter 10 for further advice.

Professional vehicle check (mechanical examination)
There are often marque/model specialists who will undertake professional examination of a vehicle on your behalf. Owners clubs will be able to put you in touch with such specialists.

Other motoring organisation with vehicle inspectors that will carry out a general professional check in the UK are:

AA – 0800 056 8040; theaa.com
RAC – 0330 159 0324; rac.co.uk
Other countries will have similar organisations

www.velocebooks.com / www.veloce.co.uk
Details of all current books • New book news • Special offers • Gift vouchers • Forum

17

6 Inspection equipment

– these items will really help

This book
Reading glasses (if you need them for close work)
Torch
Magnet (not powerful, a fridge magnet is ideal)
Probe (a small screwdriver works very well)
Overalls
Mirror on a stick
Digital camera (or smartphone)
A friend, preferably a knowledgeable enthusiast

This book is designed to be your guide at every step, so take it along, and use the check boxes to help you assess each area of the car you're interested in. Don't be afraid to let the seller see you using it.

Take your reading glasses, if you need them to read documents and make close-up inspections.

A torch with fresh batteries will be useful for peering into the wheelarches and under the car.

A magnet will help you check if the car is full of filler. Use the magnet to sample bodywork areas all around the car, but be careful not to damage the paintwork. Expect to find a little filler here and there, but not whole panels.

A small screwdriver can be used – with care – as a probe, particularly in the wheelarches and on the underside. With this you should be able to check an area of

Opening the bonnet to the upright service position will make it easier to take a close look.

If you can, get underneath the car to check for corrosion and leaks. (Courtesy MTSV)

severe corrosion, but be careful – if it's really bad, the screwdriver might go right through the metal!

Be prepared to get dirty. Take along a pair of overalls, if you have them.

Fixing a mirror at an angle on the end of a stick may seem odd, but you'll probably need it to check the condition of the underside of the car. It will also help you to peer into some of the important crevices. You can also use it, together with the torch, along the underside of the sills and on the floor.

If you have a digital camera or smartphone, take it along so that, later, you can study some areas of the car more closely. Take a picture of any part of the car that causes you concern, and seek a friend's opinion. Like the mirror on a stick, a 'selfie stick' may help you get your smartphone under the car.

Ideally, have a friend or knowledgeable enthusiast accompany you: a second opinion is always valuable.

www.velocebooks.com / www.veloce.co.uk
Details of all current books • New book news • Special offers • Gift vouchers • Forum

19

Reliable and extremely well built, the Mercedes-Benz 190 is one of the best cars you can choose as a first-time modern classic. There are still plenty of excellent cars to choose from: take your time, and be ready to move on, if the first few cars you view don't look right.

Post-face-lift cars can be recognised by their side cladding panels: check these are still in good condition. (Courtesy Mercedes-Benz Classic)

Exterior
First impressions can tell you a lot about a used car. A few minor scratches are inevitable after 25-30 years, but dented panels, parking scrapes, scuffed alloy wheels and badly worn tyres all suggest a car which has been poorly cared for. Look carefully along each side of the car for dents or uneven panels, then step back to check for mismatched paint on different parts of the body, which may be the result of poor repairs. The paintwork should be even and lustrous; red paint in particular can fade, if exposed to too much sunlight.

The 190 suffers less from corrosion than earlier Mercedes models, so serious rust should immediately be a cause for concern. Start by inspecting the front wings, the sills and jacking points, and the front and rear wheelarches. Take a look, next, at the edges of the front and rear screens, and for any milky-white signs of delamination at the edges of the glass. Are all the window and door seals still in good condition? As these dry out and perish over time, they can let water in, allowing rust to take hold, as well as causing unwanted wind noise.

Face-lifted cars (from summer 1988 onwards) were fitted with broad plastic panels at the bottom of the doors: make sure that these are secure and free from cracks, and that there is no rust bubbling around their edges.

Make sure that all the panels are well aligned, with even gaps.

The front wings of the 190 are particularly susceptible to rust.

Earlier rust has been repaired on this jacking point. (Courtesy MTSV)

Interior and boot (trunk)

The interior of the 190 is generally very durable, particularly on cars trimmed with Mercedes' legendary MB-Tex (vinyl) upholstery. Light-coloured cloth trim gives the cabin an airier feel, but is more prone to staining. Look, too, for discolouration due to water leaks, both in the footwells and around the sunroof (where fitted). High-mileage cars can be given away by wear to the driver's seat bolster, steering wheel rim, gearknob and pedal rubbers. The rare velour upholstery is less hardwearing than the other types of trim; as well as wear to the seating surfaces, check for fading on the top of the rear seat backrest, if it has been exposed to the sun.

Switch on the engine and make sure that all the instruments and warning lights operate correctly. Try each of the switches in turn, including those for the single-

blade windscreen wiper, the heater fan and radio, as well as any optional equipment fitted, such as a sunroof or electric windows.

Light-coloured cloth, like this rare Sportline beige upholstery, often shows dirt and wear.

Don't forget to look inside the boot, as it conceals one of the worst potential areas for corrosion on the 190. Lift up the mat and look under the spare wheel to check for signs of corrosion resulting from water getting in: in the most severe cases, the floor can rust right through where the towing eye is welded in place.

Do all the instruments work okay? This basic, early 190 has a large clock, rather than a rev counter. (Courtesy Mercedes-Benz Classic)

Rust in this boot floor has been patched. (Courtesy MTSV)

The engine compartment and underbody

Release the bonnet from inside the car and pull on the tongue protruding from the radiator grille to open it. You can inspect the engine more easily by raising the bonnet to the fully upright service position. Some surface corrosion on the exhaust manifolds is not a cause for concern, but make sure the manifolds are free from cracks, and that there is no rust under the battery. The engine needn't be immaculately clean, but should be free from obvious leaks. If the car has been standing, look underneath for signs of oil or other fluid leaks. Are the different hoses and the sound insulation pad in good condition, or have they dried out and cracked? Pull out the dipstick and check the oil: it should be filled to level, and be golden-brown in colour. Take off the oil filler cap and look for signs of a creamy, mayonnaise-like mix, which is often the result of head gasket failure.

Spotless engine bay on this 190E, but it has covered only 22,700 miles (36,500km).

If you can get underneath the car, have a look at the various rubber bushings and gaiters on the suspension, and for holes or excessive rust in the exhaust.

16-valve models

The 2.3-16 and 2.5-16 are exceptional sporting saloons, which sell at considerably higher prices than the other models in the range, and which are often enjoyed to the full. All the more reason, therefore, for taking special care when looking at these versions.

Refurbishing the battery tray is a commonly needed repair. (Courtesy MTSV)

All 16-valve cars came with an additional bodykit: is this still intact? Minor knocks often cause the fittings to break loose, while the front spoiler may have been scraped over speed bumps. Many of these cars are owned by enthusiasts, and may have seen hard use on-track, with the risk of accident damage, or greater mechanical wear and tear.

If the car is still fitted with the original self-levelling rear suspension, does this

Try and look under the car if you can. (Courtesy MTSV)

Sophisticated multivalve engines
fitted to the 2.3-16 and 2.5-16
need scrupulous maintenance.
(Courtesy Mercedes-Benz Classic)

Boot lid sticker suggests this car may
have been used hard on track.

operate as it should? With the engine running, the rear of the car should settle at the correct height. If, on the other hand, the suspension has been replaced, have good-quality parts been used? Have the brakes been upgraded or any other modifications made? On the 16-valve models, many enthusiasts will accept or even prefer such changes, but on the other models in the range, most collectors now prefer standard, unmodified cars.

Is it genuine and legal?

However attractive the car may look at first, it's essential that the paperwork is in order. First of all, does the VIN (the 17-digit Vehicle Identification Number) on the car tally with that on the registration/title document? On the 190, you will find the VIN on a plate riveted to the bonnet slam panel and stamped onto the right-hand secondary bulkhead at the back of the engine compartment. Make sure that the VIN hasn't been tampered with, and take a note or photograph of it for reference. You will also find an option code plate on the bonnet slam panel, which will show the options originally fitted to the car. You can look up both the VIN and option codes online to confirm the year of manufacture and exact specification of the car you are considering.

Independent organisations (see Chapter 5) will let you check that there is no finance outstanding on the car, and no record of serious accident damage. If something doesn't seem right here, walk away now. At best, you may have problems registering the car; at worst, it may be stolen or unroadworthy. Does the seller's name and address appear on the registration or title document? If you are buying privately, be sure to view the car at the owner's home address, so that you can check this tallies with the paperwork for the car.

If all these details are correct, ask to see details

VIN stamped on the
secondary bulkhead under
the bonnet.

of the car's service history, including, if possible, invoices for work done, showing the parts which have been replaced. On pre-face-lift cars, including the 2.3-16, fitted with a simplex timing chain, look for evidence that this has been changed.

If the car requires an annual roadworthiness certificate in your country (such as the MoT test in the UK), make sure that this is current, and note any advisories, indicating work that should be done. You may be able to use these to negotiate a reduction in the price you pay. Finally, make sure that the mileage on the car's odometer matches that on the service documentation or test certificates.

Road test

A road test, covering a mixture of different road types, is essential to assessing any car. Before starting off, check that you are covered by insurance, and that the indicators, lights and wipers all work.

Try and start the engine from cold, if possible: the key should turn freely in the lock, the engine should start readily, and all the warning lights should go out, including the glow plug light on the diesels. The engine should idle smoothly: on cars fitted with fuel-injection, an uneven idle may be due to air leaks in the hoses. As soon as you give the engine some revs, the oil pressure gauge should move up to its maximum reading. As you manoeuvre the car, listen for knocks or vibration on full lock, which may be due to worn engine mounts or steering rods.

The manual gearchange is naturally notchy, but the gears should engage smoothly, without any clutch slip. On cars fitted with automatic transmission, forward and reverse drive should both engage cleanly, and all changes should be smooth, whether made automatically, using kickdown in 'S' mode, or the manual override.

Keep the radio off and listen out for any untoward noises, whether undue whine from the differential, knocking sounds from the suspension, or the 'death rattle' which signals a potentially expensive timing chain failure. A rattly exhaust may mean that one section has broken loose, or that the catalytic converter (if fitted) has failed. Look in the mirror, too, for blue smoke from the exhaust, which may be the result of hardened valve stem seals, or excessive black smoke on diesels.

If you are held up in traffic, keep an eye on the water temperature gauge: the electric fan should cut in at 92° and the temperature should drop back. The 16-valve models were also fitted with an oil temperature gauge: is it still working correctly and giving a satisfactory reading? Does the speedometer needle flutter, especially at lower speeds?

On a clear stretch of open road, take your hands off the steering wheel: the car should continue to run straight. If it doesn't, an alignment check may be required. Some free play in the steering (a maximum of two fingers) is considered normal, but more than this will mean that adjustment or an overhaul of the steering will be needed.

When traffic conditions allow, apply the brakes hard: the car should pull up straight. Any judder means that the discs (rotors) are warped or corroded and should be replaced. On cars fitted with ABS, you should feel the pedal pulsing as the anti-lock system operates. Try to test the parking brake on an incline, to ensure that it will hold the car securely.

At the end of your test drive, make sure that the engine does not run on when you switch it off, and try re-starting it, now that it is completely warm.

8 Key points

– where to look for problems

Exterior
• Are all the panels straight, with even gaps?
• Is the colour and finish of the paint consistent?
• Are there signs of rust, especially on the wings, wheelarches and sills?
• Are the front and rear screens in good condition?
• Are the seals for the doors and windows in good order?
• Are the plastic body panels on 16-valve and post-face-lift cars undamaged?

Get down low to check the lower panels and underbody. (Courtesy MTSV)

Interior
• Does the overall condition of the interior match the mileage shown?
• Is the upholstery in good condition, or is it discoloured or worn?
• Are there any signs of damp under the carpets, or stains on the headlining?
• Do all the instruments and electrical equipment work correctly?
• Are there are any signs of damp or rust in the boot (trunk)?

Check the condition of the spoiler and bodykit on 16V cars. (Courtesy Mercedes-Benz Classic)

Engine and mechanicals
• How does the engine compartment look? Dirty and uncared for, or suspiciously clean?
• Are there any oil leaks or light-coloured stains where coolant has escaped?
• Are the different hoses secure and in good condition, or has the rubber perished?
• Does the car – especially 16-valve models fitted with self-levelling rear suspension – sit level?
• Are the tyres recent and in good condition?
• Is there a service history showing regular maintenance and any major work carried out?

Grey cloth interior has remained clean on this UK-market 190E. (Courtesy MTSV)

Engine bay of a 190E 2.6.

9 Serious evaluation

– 60 minutes for years of enjoyment

Score each section using the boxes as follows: 4 = excellent; 3 = good; 2 = average; 1 = poor. The totting-up procedure is detailed at the end of the chapter. Be realistic in your marking!

If you've come this far, well done! The paperwork is in order, and the car looks promising. Now is the time to take a really thorough look over it, bearing in mind the points already mentioned in the last two chapters. Try and work your way systematically around the car, so that you don't miss any details. Start outside with a close look at the bodywork, before turning your attention to the interior, and finally the engine and underbody.

Exterior

This 190E LE could pass for a three-year old car. (Courtesy MTSV)

First impressions   4   3   2   1

Make sure that you can view the car outdoors and in daylight, preferably in good weather. The car should be clean; it's hard to judge the condition of paint under a layer of dirt or dust. Begin by stepping back from the car: does it appear to sag on either side or at one end? On 2.3-16 and 2.5-16 versions fitted with self-levelling rear suspension, check, with the engine running, that this system is operating correctly. Some owners may have lowered the suspension or fitted larger wheels: do the wheels still clear the wheelarches, especially on full lock? Will the front spoiler graze the road going over speed bumps?

Bodywork   4   3   2   1

Look at the overall condition of the body: are the panels straight and crease-free, without any serious dents? When you look along the side of the car, does anything seem out of line? The panel gaps should be consistent right around the car; uneven gaps may be the result of poorly repaired accident damage. Check the roof, too, for signs of hailstone damage. On post-face-lift and 16-valve cars, check for traces of paint overspray – due to shoddy repair work – on the broad cladding panels on the lower part of the body.

Make a point of opening the boot (trunk) and each of the doors in turn: even on well-maintained cars, the seals may have hardened with age and will eventually let in moisture, allowing corrosion to take hold.

Look for even panel gaps and firmly secured cladding panels.

After at least 25 years on the road, some stone chips on the leading edge of the bonnet and scratches around the door handles are only to be expected. Have these been touched up effectively? If the paint is broken, rust can easily set in.

Overall, the paintwork should be consistent in colour and an even depth across all panels, which you can measure with a thickness gauge. Differences in adjacent areas may suggest that they have been poorly filled or that a localised respray has been carried out. Look particularly around the rear wheel arches and below the car's waistline, and examine the flat upper panels (roof, bonnet and boot lid), which may have been bleached by the sun. If the car has been resprayed in a different colour, take a look inside the engine compartment and boot: were these areas repainted at the same time?

Unlike earlier Mercedes saloons, the 190 has little chrome trim. Take a close look, though, at the radiator grille: the chrome bars and plastic slats are easily damaged, and fiddly to repair. Does the tongue to open the bonnet still pop out as it should? Does the three-pointed star still stand proudly upright?

On post-face-lift cars, the side cladding panels should be intact; cracked panels will need to be replaced. Under the front bumper (fender), the plastic cover over the front tow hook can snap off. On 16-valve models, as well as checking the bodykit parts, run your hand underneath the front spoiler to check for damage, as it may have scraped along the ground.

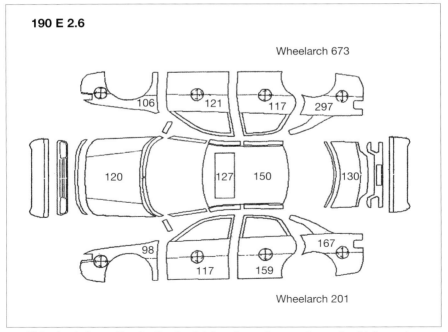

This chart shows the depth of paint (in microns) on each panel: a higher value indicates a respray. (Courtesy AixClusive Cars)

Check the condition of the three-pointed star and grille: small dents are common.

With the side cladding removed, it is easy to see if any moisture has got in, allowing rust to develop.

Plastic cover over the front towing eye: easily broken off or lost.

Body corrosion

The W201 is much less prone to corrosion than the W123 model which preceded it, with better-quality steel and galvanised body panels, extensive wax protection and a design which had fewer natural rust traps. It has also fared better than the W202

This front wing is already badly rusted and will need to be replaced. (Courtesy MTSV)

The rear wheelarch extension has been removed on this 16-valve car and the wheelarch is being restored. (Courtesy MTSV)

Severe corrosion has taken hold around this jacking point. (Courtesy MTSV)

The paint is easily damaged if the radio aerial has to be replaced, allowing the formation of rust to begin.

(the first 'C-Class' Mercedes) which replaced it. Inevitably, as with any car of this age, rust can occur in many places, but in most cases, this can be treated at an early stage. The UK Mercedes-Benz Club has some excellent archive features on dealing with these issues.

The earliest cars (built from 1983-85) are generally more liable to corrosion than later cars, but do have the advantage of a simple rubbing strip on each side rather than the larger cladding panels fitted to post-face-lift cars: rust can begin to form under these panels and will only become apparent when blisters start to form along the top. The bodykit fitted to the 16-valve models is also the source of additional problems: water can get trapped behind the rear wheelarch extensions, allowing the wheelarches to rust away undetected.

Start your examination by looking at the lower part of the body: at the bottom of the doors, under the wheelarches (check for bubbling around the rubber seals), and at the base of the front wings. Use a torch to get a better view inside the wheelarches. The front wings bolt on, but are expensive to replace (●x640). The mounting bracket securing the front of the inner wing liner and the bumper side bolt can also rust.

As with all Mercedes of this era, the jacking points should be checked (remove the bungs or the plastic covers on post-face-lift cars): not only can the points themselves rust, but they are a valuable guide to the overall condition of the sills. If you have any doubts, ask the seller if you can use the jack to lift the car and test the solidity of each jacking point. If too far gone, these can lead to failure in a UK MoT test or other similar safety inspection.

Now check the edges of the front and rear screens. The front windscreen is glued in place, and leaks are therefore rare. Corrosion is most likely to occur if the screen has been replaced and badly fitted, damaging the paintwork. The rear screen, on the other hand, uses a traditional rubber seal, which shrinks over time. This can allow moisture to creep in and cause corrosion around the edges of the screen; water can also get into the boot.

A few other areas should also be checked on the outside of the car: along the edge of the boot lid, around the fuel filler, boot lock and number (license) plate lights, and at the base of the radio aerial (antenna), especially if the aerial has been replaced. On any cars with a rear spoiler, check where this is attached to the boot lid.

Standard plastic hubcap on pre-face-lift car; note the rubber bung covering the jacking point.

This alloy wheel is showing only very minor corrosion and kerbing damage.

Wheels

To match its new, modern styling, the 190 abandoned Mercedes' traditional painted hubcaps in favour of simply styled plastic wheel trims. These look rather plain, but are easy to replace if cracked or scratched. The 16-valve and Sportline cars were fitted with 15-hole alloy wheels, which were also an option on the other models in the range. At the end of the 190's life, an 8-hole alloy wheel became available, which is easier to keep clean. The alloy wheels fitted to the very first cars in 1983 were subject to a recall in the US due to possible cracking, but otherwise there are few problems to note. Like any alloy wheels, those fitted to the 190 can go dull over time or suffer kerbing damage, but refurbishing them is a straightforward job for any wheel specialist.

On the 16-valve models, avoid larger than standard wheels (only the Evo and Evo II models went above 15in rims), which are often combined with lowered suspension. These can cause damage to the driveshafts and hub bearings.

Glass

4 3 2 1

Examine the windscreen, side windows and rear screen in turn. If any of the windows have been tinted, is the depth of tint within the legally allowable limits in your country? Is the film showing any signs of cracks or lifting off?

The condition of the windscreen is especially important, as it is most vulnerable to damage from stone chips. A crack in the driver's line of sight may cause the car to fail a roadworthiness inspection, such as the MoT test in the UK. The windscreen is prone to scratching from the big panoramic wiper; as the glass used on the W201 is relatively thin, scratches can be hard to polish out, and a replacement (which costs about ⬤x300) may be the only cure.

Both front and rear screens may appear milky-white at the bottom or around the edges: this is the result of delamination, which can occur if the frame has corroded.

Check for tell-tale signs of leaks around the screens: corrosion around the frame or milky traces on the glass.

Interior
First impressions

4 3 2 1

The interior of the 190 is very durable, and, with a little TLC, it should go on looking good. Take a look, first, at the steering wheel, gear knob and pedal rubbers: if these seem shiny and heavily worn, the car has probably covered a high mileage – does that tally with the distance showing on the odometer? Interiors trimmed in light-coloured cloth can stain easily; darker colours and leather or MB-Tex (vinyl) upholstery are more resistant to everyday wear and tear. If the car smells damp when you open the door, it is very likely that water has made its way in: lift the carpets and look for signs of rust on the floorpan, and raise the rear seat squab, as water can collect beneath it.

Light-coloured cloth shows dirt and signs of wear more readily.

Grey MB-Tex looks austere, but is virtually indestructible.

After nearly 200,000 miles (320,000km), this driver's seat shows remarkably little wear. (Courtesy Mercedes-Benz UK)

Velour trim looks luxurious, but wears less well, especially at the edges.

Upholstery and trim   ☐4 ☐3 ☐2 ☐1

Some passengers may find the seats on the 190 too firm for their liking, but in general, they should last as well as the rest of the car. The driver's seat may, however, sag at high mileages, while the front centre armrest can collapse if too much weight is applied to it. As on many cars, the side bolster on the driver's seat is prone to wear; on cars with the optional velour upholstery, this is even more likely, as the 190 did not have the ribbed outer sections fitted to the velour seats in the W123 or S-Class models. On 16-valve models or cars fitted with the optional part-leather Sportline trim, inspect the seams where the cloth and leather meet, as these can come undone.

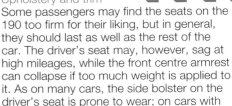

Check seams on Sportline-style seats.

The trim inside the 190 is held in place with countless plastic clips, which gradually become brittle and snap, especially if a part has to be removed and refitted. On the car you are viewing, are all the door cards and the panels on the outer sides of the front seats (on post-face-lift cars) secure? Can you open and close the glovebox lid? The door trim tends to come unstuck along its upper edge, as the material shrinks over time. Cars exposed to too much sunlight can suffer from cracked dashboard tops, especially those finished in blue.

Boot (trunk)   ☐4 ☐3 ☐2 ☐1

Corrosion caused by water getting in is the bugbear here. First, remove the carpet (does it have any residual stains?) and spare wheel, and examine the condition of the floor, including the spare wheel well. The boot floor has a double-skinned construction and the towing eye was originally welded into this structure. If water gets in between the different layers of metal, the floor can eventually rust right through. As it is near one of the suspension mounting points, this will certainly lead to the car failing its MoT or other safety inspection. The second critical point to check is for signs of damp under the rear parcel shelf: the roof pillar, wing, and a strengthening section are all soldered together at one point, which is key to the car's structural integrity.

Other leaks into the boot can occur from the rear screen, the boot lock, or via the C-pillar vents, if the rubber seals there perish. The three-pointed star on the boot lid is another potential culprit: if you suspect that water has found its way inside the boot lid, there is a tiny bung at the left-hand corner of the lid which you can remove to let water drain out.

Make a point of pulling out the plastic wing liners inside the boot: water can settle at the bottom of the side wells, especially on the left-hand side, if it has got past the radio aerial base. Make sure that the drain holes at the bottom of the side wells are unobstructed. With the right-hand liner removed, also check the emergency fuel flap release: pull on the red knob at the end of the cable, but be warned that this can become brittle over time, and simply snap off.

Finally, check that all the equipment is present and correct, including the spare wheel, warning triangle (clipped inside the boot lid), jack and tool kit.

A classic case of a boot floor which has rusted around the towing eye. (Courtesy MTSV)

The spare wheel well on this car has been welded to deal with earlier corrosion. (Courtesy MTSV)

Electrics
Instruments and controls

As you settle into the car, check that both front seats adjust as they should. Try opening each of the windows in turn: on manual windows, the cables can break, while the wiring for electric windows can shear between the pillar and the door.

At high mileages (typically over 150,000 miles/240,000km), the ignition lock barrel can fail: in the worst cases, the key will break off in the barrel and it will be impossible to turn it. If the lock is reluctant to turn, this is a first indication of this impending problem. Assuming that the ignition lock is working correctly, and before starting the engine, make sure that the charge warning light comes on (and then goes out, once the engine is running). The warning lamps for low fuel and low oil may come on when the levels are, in fact, correct: sometimes this problem can be fixed with an inexpensive replacement transistor, rather than changing the entire printed circuit board.

On pre-face-lift cars especially, the VDO speedometer can fail. The main and trip distance recorders can also jam, often as a result of resetting the trip meter to zero when the car is moving. If the unit has been replaced, the mileage showing may not be the total distance the car has covered: look for wear on the steering wheel, gear knob and seat bolsters, or frayed seatbelts, which may indicate a higher real mileage. On cars left in the sun, the instrument needles tend to fade from orange to yellow. If the speedometer needle flickers, this can often be fixed

The 190 had a comprehensive set of instruments; do they all still work?

Optional outside temperature gauge has begun to bleed from the left-hand edge.

Plenty of extras to check on this 2.5-16: heated front seats, electric passenger door mirror, stereo fader, and four electric windows.

by greasing the cable. A flickering fuel gauge needle, on the other hand, particularly over the last quarter, may be caused by a faulty sender (a simple fix) or potentiometer. The oil pressure gauge should move up to its maximum (3 bar) as soon as you give the engine some revs. If the car you are viewing has an outside temperature gauge, the display may 'bleed' at the edges and will eventually become unreadable. On the 16-valve versions, the clock/stopwatch in the centre console can also suffer from depixellation. Finally, check that the instrument lighting works as it should.

Mercedes pioneered its unique single-blade windscreen wiper on the W201, with a 'jumping' mechanism to ensure it covered 86% of the glass area. If the blade judders or fails to park properly, the mechanism will need to be greased (with graphite oil), a service job which is often overlooked. If the wiper mechanism fails to work correctly, it can overload the combination switch for the lights, wipers and indicators. It is worth testing the windscreen washer as well, as the pump bearings can run dry, if they are not lubricated regularly.

Make a point of operating the heater fan at all speeds; if it emits a high-pitched squeal, it may be on its last legs. Incidentally, the central dash vents always blow air at ambient temperature, to provide fresh air at face level. The vents themselves are quite fragile and their vanes can snap, especially if they are used to support the holder for a mobile phone, while the control knobs for the heater fan and air-conditioning can break off.

Any optional equipment fitted should be tested, including the cruise control (an important safety consideration), electric sunroof, headlamp wipers and alarm. The exterior door mirror was electrically operated only on the passenger side: check that it adjusts in both planes, as the plastic clips securing the glass can break or the mechanism jam. This may be considered a safety issue in statutory roadworthiness inspections, such as the British MoT test.

Audio systems

Mercedes originally specified high-quality Becker radios and radio-cassette players as options on the 190, and these are now highly sought-after. In the UK, the late-model LE had a Blaupunkt Verona unit. Make sure that any radio fitted works as

Original Becker Grand Prix radio-cassette player, with sliding control for air-conditioning above it.

On this radio aerial, one section has jammed.

it should, and that the electric aerial extends and retracts correctly: it tends to stick halfway, but can often be freed with some WD40®. The quality of the original speakers is rather poor, but if they have been replaced, look for damage to the door cards or rear parcel shelf. The front-to-rear fader was controlled by a thumbwheel on the centre console: if this is fitted, make sure it is still working. A mobile phone holder may also have left marks on the centre console.

Lights
4 3 2 1

There are no particular issues to worry about for the lights fitted to the 190. At the

Ribbed taillamps typical of Mercedes-Benz vehicles of the period.

front, check that the reflectors and lenses are clear; proprietary cleaning products can often revive lenses which have become cloudy. The taillamps had a special ribbed design to keep them clean in bad weather: make sure that they are free from cracks. Any failed bulbs can easily be changed from inside the boot, by undoing the knurled knob on the panel behind the taillamp assembly.

Keeping cool: sunroof and air-conditioning
4 3 2 1

Score four points if not fitted: one less thing to cause problems!

On cars fitted with a sunroof, check that it can be raised into the tilt position, and that it opens and closes smoothly (the rails need to be greased regularly). If it fails to open correctly, the problem may be a snapped cable or a stripped cog in the motor. Look for stains on the headlining: if the drainage tubes have become blocked or are disconnected, water will leak around the roof and into the boot or the cabin (via the A-pillars).

Air-conditioning is an unusual luxury on a compact European saloon from this period. The OEM (Behr) system fitted to the 190 used R12 refrigerant, which has now been banned. Substitutes such as Duracool do exist, so you may still be able to use the original system, if it is continuing to operate correctly. If the air-conditioning is not blowing properly cold air, however, and a simple recharge is not enough, you will need to overhaul the system so that it can use the now-current R134-a refrigerant. This is an expensive job which must be performed by an A/C specialist (potentially costing up to ●x800). The seals and pipes will need to be replaced; after 25 years or more, it is very likely that the expansion

Look for signs of water damage on the sunroof headlining.

valve, condenser and compressor will need to be overhauled as well. In the US, some cars were fitted with a more elaborate climate control system. This is more complex to repair, as it requires stripping out the entire dashboard.

Battery

☐4☐ ☐3☐ ☐2☐ ☐1☐

The battery on the 190 is sandwiched between the two parts of the bulkhead at

the rear of the engine compartment. Look for signs of corrosion underneath it, which can be caused if acid seeps out of it. You will need a multimeter to check its condition. If in doubt, ask the seller when the battery was last changed and, if necessary, budget on getting a new one. A trickle charger is also a wise investment, to keep the battery in good condition, especially if you only plan on using the car occasionally.

Take a look at the fuse box at the same time, as water can leak into it. If cleaning any fuses does not resolve an electrical problem, they are easy to change, as are the two relays for the fuel

Battery should be recent, and to correct specification.

pump and the overload protection for the fuel-injection system.

Engine and mechanicals

Under the bonnet (hood): first impressions

☐4☐ ☐3☐ ☐2☐ ☐1☐

In common with many Mercedes-Benz models of the period, the bonnet can be lifted to a special service position at 90 degrees, which gives great access to the engine. Take a look at the overall condition of the engine bay: are all the belts and hoses secure and free from cracks or other damage? The soundproofing under the bonnet often disintegrates over the years: it looks unsightly, but is inexpensive to replace. Are there any traces of oil or other fluid leaks? The plastic expansion tank can crack, causing the coolant to seep out. If the fuel lines have leaked, you may smell fuel around the engine.

With the bonnet fully raised, the condition of the insulation pad can easily be checked.

No worries here: mild surface corrosion on manifolds, and no oil leaks. (Courtesy AixClusive Cars)

Can you see any rust? Surface corrosion on the exhaust manifolds is not usually serious, but take a look at the bottom of the radiator, under the headlamps, and at the secondary bulkhead sections: owners sometimes neglect to clear these out, allowing leaves and moisture to accumulate. If left untreated, water can end up leaking into the footwells. Check for rust, too, under the windscreen washer reservoir and around the suspension top mounts: repairs to these can be expensive.

General mechanical issues

4 3 2 1

The engines, transmission and suspension fitted to the 190 have a good reputation for their solid, long-lived construction. A full engine overhaul will be expensive, however, so it is worth taking your time to look at the car's service history, and to listen for undue noises on test, especially given the high mileages many of these cars will have covered. Scored pistons, for example, may show up as a clicking noise, which becomes louder as the engine speed increases. A periodic misfire, on the other hand, may be nothing more than a faulty distributor cap: these should be replaced on a preventive basis every 30,000 miles (50,000km).

Does the radiator core appear intact? On all models, the cooling system needs regular changes of coolant to ensure it continues to work well and prevent damage to the alloy head; if neglected, this can eventually lead to cracks in the engine block. Over time, the engine mounts can wear: knocking and vibration with the steering on full lock can give this away.

Scoring: score *one* of the following four sections (on the usual 4-3-2-1 scale) depending on which engine is fitted to the car you are assessing.

Four-cylinder petrol engines

4 3 2 1

Of the different four-cylinder models, the 2.0-litre 190E is probably the best all-round bet. The Pierburg 2E2 carburettor fitted to some basic 190 models is complex and difficult to set up well. Look out for an uneven idle or the smell of unburned fuel from the exhaust. The later 190E 1.8 version is smoother but rather uninspiring, with modest performance and unexceptional fuel economy. The fuel-injected 2.0 and 2.3 models offer better performance, but should also be checked for uneven running. The 2.3 cannot be retrofitted with a catalytic converter, which may become an issue in areas where exhaust emissions are ever more tightly controlled.

Like the W123 models fitted with the same M102 engine, the simplex timing chain on early cars can fail. You can check which type is fitted by removing the oil filler cap and looking underneath. Listen for the characteristic 'death rattle' of a failing chain, and look at the service history of the car you are viewing to know when it was last changed: this should be done every 60,000 miles (100,000km). After 1987, the engines were fitted with a much stronger and more reliable double-row riming chain.

This well-worn 190E will need a thorough mechanical inspection. (Courtesy Mercedes-Benz UK)

On all models, watch for oil leaks around the rocker cover at the top of the engine or unexplained coolant loss, resulting from the failure of the cylinder head gasket.

16-valve petrol engines

   [1]

The high-performance engines in the 2.3-16 and 2.5-16 are very different from those fitted to the 'cooking' versions of the 190. If over-revved (on track days, for example), damage to the bores and valves may occur.

Early in the life of the 2.3-16, problems occurred with cracked exhaust manifolds on right-hand drive cars, due to their weight and convoluted design, causing them to break free from their mounts. Many were dealt with by Mercedes-Benz under warranty, but the part is no longer available, so cracked manifolds can now only be welded or replaced with a secondhand part.

A more common, and potentially serious, issue on the 2.3-16 is with the simplex timing chain, which needs to be replaced (together with the tensioners)

every 60,000 miles (100,000km). If neglected, the chain can break free, resulting in serious damage to the cylinder head and valves. Be sure, therefore, to look for invoices to show that this maintenance work has been carried out.

The 2.5-16 was fitted with a duplex timing chain, which is much stronger and causes fewer problems. It also suffers from fewer problems with hardened valve stem seals, denoted by blue smoke from the exhaust on the overrun.

The timing chain on the 2.3-16: regular replacement is essential. (Courtesy Mercedes-Benz Classic)

Six-cylinder petrol engines

Unlike some of the six-cylinder W124 and R129 models, there are no biodegradable wiring looms to worry about on the 190E 2.6. If you notice signs of oil leaks around the cylinder head, however, a new cylinder head gasket and oil seals may be needed. As on the 2.3-16, blue smoke from the exhaust is typically the result of hardened valve stem seals, which will need to be replaced, a job best left to professionals or advanced home mechanics. There have been some cases of the thermostat and water pump failing at higher mileages, but these are relatively straightforward to replace.

The cylinder head gasket and oil seals are being replaced on this 190E 2.6. (Courtesy AixClusive Cars)

Diesel engines

The diesel engines fitted to the 190 are exceptionally long-lived, with half-a-million miles not uncommon. At high mileages, however, the vacuum pump is prone to failure, as is the accessory belt drive tensioner. If you see excessive black smoke from the exhaust during a test drive, this may be the result of faults in the fuel-injection system, although defective injector nozzles are easy to fix.

Like other diesels of its time, the 190 uses glow plugs at start-up: if the warning light remains off when turning the key to the accessory position, but comes on for ten seconds after starting the engine, one or more of the glow plugs has failed. The parts themselves are cheap to replace, but two of them are awkward to get at. The UK Mercedes-Benz Club has archived a feature on carrying out this job yourself.

The OM601 engine fitted to the 190D. (Courtesy Mercedes-Benz Classic)

Exhaust system

Try to get a good look at the condition of the exhaust from underneath the car. The welds on the tail section of the exhaust can fail; individual replacement sections are easy to find and not too expensive, at least on cars without catalytic converters. The latter are much more expensive (over ●x500 for a complete system from Mercedes-Benz), so check for rattling sounds from the exhaust, which may indicate that the system has failed. On 16-valve models, a broken exhaust downpipe will cause a loss of power and more noise when running.

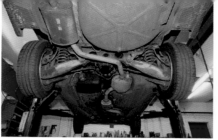

If you can, check the full length of the exhaust system from underneath the car. (Courtesy MTSV)

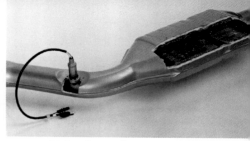

Listen for rattling noises from the catalytic converter. (Courtesy Mercedes-Benz Classic)

Transmission

Scoring: score *one* of the following two sections (on the usual 4-3-2-1 scale) depending on whether the car you are assessing is fitted with manual or automatic transmission.

Straightforward manual gearchange and central parking brake. (Courtesy Mercedes-Benz Classic)

Manual transmission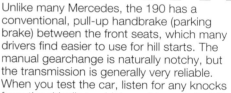

Unlike many Mercedes, the 190 has a conventional, pull-up handbrake (parking brake) between the front seats, which many drivers find easier to use for hill starts. The manual gearchange is naturally notchy, but the transmission is generally very reliable. When you test the car, listen for any knocks from the driveline, which could mean that the propshaft discs or bearings need changing. Look underneath the differential: slight weeping is normal, but more significant oil leaks should be investigated.

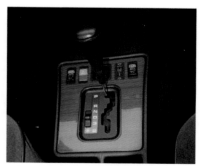

Mercedes' traditional stepped gate for the automatic gear selector, and choice of 'S' and 'E' modes.

Automatic transmission

Mercedes' automatics were long considered the best in the business, and the four-speed transmission fitted to the 190 is no exception. All changes, whether automatic, manual or under kickdown (in 'S' mode) should go through smoothly. Don't be surprised, however, if the car (especially the less powerful versions) feels sluggish when starting off, as it is set up to start in second in normal driving.

If you sense a clunk when moving from Drive to Reverse, this may be caused by a fault with the differential or the failure of the plastic bushings in the transmission selector mechanism, which disintegrate over time. The latter are very cheap to replace (●x15), but refitting them requires an extensive strip-down taking several hours.

Suspension

With the exception of the 2.3-16 and 2.5-16, the suspension on the 190 is conventional and long-lived, and replacement parts are readily available. As with any car, however, the 190's suspension components do wear out over time, and excessive wear or damage to the steering or suspension can lead, in turn, to increased or uneven tyre wear. Especially on cars which have covered over 100,000 miles (160,000km), a thorough check of the front and rear suspension is important: this should include the front and rear suspension mounts, front suspension struts, lower ball joints, and bushes. Look for excessive free play and corrosion on the different components, and for perished rubber sleeves.

Sophisticated rear suspension on all 190 models. (Courtesy Mercedes-Benz Classic)

Check for cracked springs and corrosion on the suspension. (Courtesy MTSV)

16-valve cars were originally fitted as standard with self-levelling rear suspension. This is more complex to maintain than the conventional set-up, with fluid leaks from the system making the suspension feel excessively hard. Faults also arise with the pressure accumulators and suspension pumps (which are no longer available new). As a result, many owners have reverted to conventional rear suspension, using Sportline or aftermarket components, the latter sometimes optimised for track use.

Steering

The 190 uses a relatively old-fashioned recirculating ball system; a small amount of play around the straight-ahead position is normal, but if it is excessive, the car will fail a safety inspection, such as the MoT test in the UK. Some adjustment of the steering box is possible, but in the worst cases, a replacement may be required. Kerbing can also damage the steering system: another reason for looking carefully at the condition of the wheel rims on any car you are considering.

Large steering wheel, typical of Mercedes' cars of the time. (Courtesy MTSV)

When you test the car, listen for any knocking sounds when you apply lock, which may suggest that the steering rods need to be replaced. From underneath the car, check the condition of the rubber sleeves, which naturally perish and crack: these are straightforward and inexpensive to change. Look, too, for any leaks from the steering damper.

On the vast majority of cars equipped with power steering, the system has a tiny filter, which should be changed every 12,000 miles (20,000km), a job often overlooked. Can you see any evidence, in the car's service history, that this has been done recently?

Tyres

Ideally, the car you are viewing should be fitted with a matching set of tyres from a reputable brand, with plenty of tread. Don't forget to check the spare tyre in the boot, as well. The date of manufacture of the tyres is important, too, as rubber hardens over time, making the tyres less responsive and ultimately liable to cracking. If the tyres on the car you are examining are worn down to a tread depth of 3mm or less, or are more than five years old (which you can verify by checking the DOT code on the sidewall), they will need to be replaced. This is a cost you can often use as a bargaining tool, if the car otherwise looks good.

Correct tyre pressures were originally shown inside the fuel flap.

Applying copper grease to protect the brake lines.

Brakes

All models of the 190 were fitted with disc brakes all round, and dual braking circuits. The system presents few notable issues, and both pads and discs (rotors) are reasonably priced when replacements are needed. Turning the front wheels from side to side will give you a better view of the condition of the pads; the design of the plastic wheel trims and alloy wheels means, however, that you will only be able to check the condition of the discs by removing the wheels. If that is not possible, is there a recent invoice for a brake service with the car?

Vacuum system

Like other Mercedes-Benz cars from this era, the 190 was fitted with a vacuum-operated central locking system, covering all doors, the boot and fuel flap. Some problems have been reported on pre-face-lift cars, so be sure to test the system. A momentary delay in the time at which each door unlocks is perfectly normal. If the fuel flap initially fails to open when the car is parked, try starting the engine to obtain enough pressure to operate it. The vacuum pump itself is generally reliable, and faults are more often the result of a leaking hose.

A thorough underbody examination is essential when buying a car of this age. (Courtesy MTSV)

Drainage hole from the windscreen should be kept clear.

The chassis should appear straight: if it looks out of alignment, that should alert you to the possibility of accident damage. Beware of cars which have a thick, or very recent, coat of underseal, which may be hiding a multitude of sins. Gently tap the underside of the car with a screwdriver to make sure that the metal is solid. The front and rear subframes, in particular, can rust badly. Cars from areas with hard winters may have suffered from salt applied to the roads, if this has not been regularly washed off. Check, too, that the drain hole from the windscreen behind the front wheel is clear.

While underneath the car, inspect the fuel and brake lines to ensure they are free from damage. The brake lines can be treated with copper grease (using a paintbrush) to keep them in good condition. On cars with automatic transmission, a gearbox oil cooling pipe runs underneath the radiator to the front of the gearbox: it is exposed to damp and dirt, and can eventually rust through, with the risk of serious damage to the gearbox. Replacing it is a relatively cheap precautionary measure.

Professional inspection

Having your car inspected by a Mercedes specialist can often be a sound investment, giving you extra peace of mind when buying a good car ... and maybe saving you from buying a 'bad 'un.' No genuine seller should object to this, provided, of course, that you cover any costs involved. A professional should be able to inspect the car on a lift, and have access to specialised equipment (to carry out a compression test, for example).

Evaluation procedure

Add up the total points from each section.
Score: 100 = perfect; 75 = good; 50 = average; 25 = buyer beware! Cars scoring over 75 should be completely usable, and require the minimum of repair or rectification, although continued service maintenance and care will be required to keep them in good condition. Cars scoring between 50 and 74 will require serious work (at much the same cost regardless of score). Cars scoring between 25 and 49 will require very careful assessment of the repair costs needed.

10 Auctions
– sold! Another way to buy your dream

Auction pros & cons
Pros: Prices are often lower than those of dealers or private sellers, and you might grab a real bargain on the day. Auctioneers have generally established clear title with the seller. At the venue, you can usually examine documentation relating to the vehicle.

Cons: You have to rely on a sketchy catalogue description of condition and history. The opportunity to inspect is limited and you cannot drive the car. Auction cars are often a little below par and may require some work. It's easy to overbid. There will usually be a buyer's premium to pay, in addition to the auction hammer price.

Which auction?
Auctions by established auctioneers are advertised in car magazines and on the auction houses' websites. A catalogue, or a simple printed list of the lots for auctions, might only be available a day or two ahead, though often lots are listed and pictured on auctioneers' websites much earlier. Contact the auction company to ask if previous auction selling prices are available, as this is useful information (details of past sales are often available on websites).

Catalogue, entry fee, and payment details
When you purchase the catalogue of vehicles in an auction, it often acts as a ticket allowing two people to attend the viewing days and the auction. Catalogue details tend to be comparatively brief, but will include information such as 'one owner from new, low mileage, full service history,' etc. It will also usually show a guide price to give you some idea of what to expect to pay, and will tell you what is charged as a 'Buyer's premium.' The catalogue will also contain details of acceptable forms of payment. At the fall of the hammer, an immediate deposit is usually required, the balance payable within 24 hours. If the plan is to pay by cash, there may be a cash limit. Some auctions will accept payment by debit card. Sometimes credit or charge cards are acceptable, but will often incur an extra charge. A bank draft or bank transfer will have to be arranged in advance with your own bank as well as with the auction house. No car will be released before all payments are cleared. If delays occur in payment transfers, then storage costs can accrue.

Buyer's premium
A buyer's premium will be added to the hammer price: don't forget this in your calculations. It is not usual for there to be a further state tax or local tax on the purchase price and/or on the buyer's premium.

Viewing
In some instances, it's possible to view on the day, or days before, as well as in the hours prior to, the auction. There are auction officials available who are willing to help out by opening engine and luggage compartments and to allow you to inspect the interior. While the officials may start the engine for you, a test drive is out of the question. Crawling under and around the car as much as you want is permitted, but

you can't suggest that the car you are interested in be jacked up, or attempt to do the job yourself. You can also ask to see any documentation available.

Bidding
Before you take part in the auction, decide your maximum bid – and stick to it!

It may take a while for the auctioneer to reach the lot you are interested in, so use that time to observe how other bidders behave. When it's the turn of your car, attract the auctioneer's attention and make an early bid. The auctioneer will then look to you for a reaction every time another bid is made, usually the bids will be in fixed increments until the bidding slows, when smaller increments will often be accepted before the hammer falls. If you want to withdraw from the bidding, make sure the auctioneer understands your intentions – a vigorous shake of the head when he or she looks to you for the next bid should do the trick!

Assuming that you are the successful bidder, the auctioneer will note your card or paddle number, and, from that moment on, you will be responsible for the vehicle.

If the car is unsold, either because it failed to reach the reserve or because there was little interest, it may be possible to negotiate with the owner, via the auctioneers, after the sale is over.

Successful bid
There are two more items to think about. How to get the car home, and insurance. If you can't drive the car, your own or a hired trailer is one way, another is to have the vehicle shipped using the facilities of a local company. The auction house will also have details of companies specialising in the transfer of cars.

Insurance for immediate cover can usually be purchased on site, but it may be more cost-effective to make arrangements with your own insurance company in advance, and then call to confirm the full details.

eBay and other online auctions
eBay and other online auctions could land you a car at a bargain price, though you'd be foolhardy to bid without examining the car first, something most vendors encourage. A useful feature of eBay is that the geographical location of the car is shown, so you can narrow your choices to those within a realistic radius of home. Be prepared to be outbid in the last few moments of the auction. Remember, your bid is binding and that it will be very, very difficult to get restitution in the case of a crooked vendor fleecing you – *caveat emptor!*

Be aware that some cars offered for sale in online auctions are 'ghost' cars. Don't part with any cash without being sure that the vehicle actually exists, and is as described (usually pre-bidding inspection is possible).

Auctioneers
Barrett-Jackson www.barrett-jackson.com/ **Bonhams** www.bonhams.com/ **British Car Auctions BCA)** www.bca-europe.com or www.british-car-auctions. co.uk/ **Christies** www.christies.com/ **Coys** www.coys.co.uk/ **eBay** www.eBay. com/ **H&H** www.handh.co.uk/ **RM Sotheby's** www.rmsothebys.com/ **Shannons** www.shannons.com.au/ **Silver** www.silverauctions.com.

11 Paperwork
– correct documentation is essential!

The paper trail

Enthusiasts' cars often come with a large portfolio of paperwork accumulated by a succession of proud owners. This documentation represents the real history of the car, and shows the level of care the car has received, how it's been used, which specialists have worked on it and the dates of major repairs.

Registration documents

All countries/states have some form of registration for private vehicles, whether it's like the American 'pink slip' system or the British 'log book' system.

It is essential to check that the registration document is genuine, that it relates to the car in question, and that all the vehicle's details are correctly recorded, including chassis/VIN and engine numbers (if these are shown). If you are buying from the previous owner, his or her name and address will be recorded in the document; this will not be the case if you are buying from a dealer.

In the UK, the current (Euro-aligned) registration document is named 'V5C,' and is printed in coloured sections of blue, green and pink. The blue section relates to the car specification, the green section has details of the new owner and the pink section is sent to the DVLA in the UK when the car is sold. A small section in yellow deals with selling the car within the motor trade.

In the UK, the DVLA will provide details of earlier keepers of the vehicle, upon payment of a small fee, and much can be learned in this way.

If the car has a foreign registration, there may be expensive and time-consuming formalities to complete. Do you really want the hassle?

Roadworthiness certificate

Most country/state administrations require that vehicles are regularly tested to prove that they are safe to use on the public highway and do not produce excessive emissions. In the UK, that test (the 'MoT') is carried out at approved testing stations, for a fee. In the US, the requirement varies, but most states insist on an emissions test every two years as a minimum, while the police are charged with pulling over unsafe-looking vehicles.

In the UK, the test is required on an annual basis once a vehicle becomes three years old. Of particular relevance for older cars is that the certificate issued includes the mileage reading recorded at the test date and, therefore, becomes an independent record of that car's history. Ask the seller if previous certificates are available. Without an MoT, the vehicle should be trailered to its new home, unless you insist that a valid MoT is part of the deal. (Not such a bad idea this, as at least you will know the car was roadworthy on the day it was tested and you don't need to wait for the old certificate to expire before having the test done.)

Road licence

The administration of nearly every country/state charges some kind of tax for the use of its road system, the actual form of the 'road licence' and, how it is displayed, varying enormously country to country and state to state.

Whatever the form of the 'road licence,' it must relate to the vehicle carrying it and must be present and valid if the car is to be driven on the public highway legally. The value of the licence will depend on the length of time it will continue to be valid.

Changed legislation in the UK means that the seller of a car must surrender any existing road fund licence, and it is the responsibility of the new owner to re-tax the vehicle at the time of purchase and before the car can be driven on the road. It's therefore vital to see the Vehicle Registration Certificate (V5C) at the time of purchase, and to have access to the New Keeper Supplement (V5C/2), allowing the buyer to obtain road tax immediately.

If the car is untaxed because it has not been used for a period of time, the owner has to inform the licensing authorities, otherwise the vehicle's date-related registration number will be lost and there will be a painful amount of paperwork to get it re-registered.

Valuation certificate

A private vendor may have a recent valuation certificate, or letter signed by a recognised expert stating how much he, or she, believes the particular car to be worth (such documents, together with photos, are usually needed to get 'agreed value' insurance). Generally, such documents should act only as confirmation of your own assessment of the car rather than a guarantee of value. The easiest way to find out how to obtain a formal valuation is to contact the owners' club.

Data cards and VIN/engine numbers

Each Mercedes left the factory with a detailed data card, specifying the exact model, colour and trim, and the codes for each option fitted. These codes – which you can look up on many online sites – should correspond to the actual equipment on the car you are viewing, and provide valuable confirmation of its authenticity. If the card is missing, Mercedes-Benz' Classic department in your country may be able to supply a replacement. These codes are repeated on the stamped metal plate on the bonnet slam panel.

The 17-digit VIN (Vehicle Identification Number) on the data card should tally with that on the car, which you can find on a plate on the bonnet slam panel and stamped on the bulkhead separating the battery compartment from the engine bay.

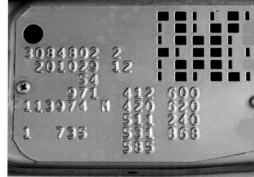

Data card for the author's own 190E 2.6.

Options code plate at the front of the engine should match the data card.

The engine number is stamped on the side of the cylinder block: this is particularly worth checking on the 2.3-16 and 2.5-16 models.

For cars with some models of Becker radio, you may also find a safety code card with the re-set code to be used in an emergency.

Service history

Try to obtain as much service history and other paperwork pertaining to the car as you can. Naturally, dealer stamps, or specialist garage receipts score most points in the value stakes. However, anything helps in the great authenticity game, items like the original bill of sale, handbook, parts invoices and repair bills adding to the story and the character of the car. Even a brochure correct to the year of the car's manufacture is a useful document and something that you could well have to search hard to locate in future years. If the seller claims that the car has been restored, then expect receipts and other evidence from a specialist restorer.

A stamped-up service booklet will provide reassurance that the car has been regularly maintained.

If the seller claims to have carried out regular servicing at home, ask what work was completed and when, and seek some evidence of it being carried out. Your assessment of the car's overall condition should tell you whether the seller's claims are genuine.

Restoration photographs

If the seller tells you that the car has undergone significant work, ask to be shown a series of photographs taken while the work was under way. These should help you gauge the thoroughness of the work. If you buy the car, ask if you can have all the photographs, as they form an important part of the vehicle's history. It's surprising how many sellers are happy to part with their car and accept your cash, but want to hang on to their photographs! In the latter event, you may be able to persuade the vendor to get a set of copies made.

Previous ownership records

Due to the introduction of important new legislation on data protection, it is no longer possible to acquire, from the British DVLA, a list of previous owners of a car you own, or are intending to purchase. This scenario will also apply to dealerships, and other specialists, whom you may wish to contact to acquire information on previous ownership and work carried out.

www.velocebooks.com / www.veloce.co.uk
Details of all current books • New book news • Special offers • Gift vouchers • Forum

48

12 What's it worth?
– let your head rule your heart

Condition

If the car you've been looking at is really bad, then you've probably not bothered to use the marking system in Chapter 9 – 60-minute evaluation. You may not have even got as far as using that chapter at all!

If you did use the marking system in Chapter 9, you'll know whether the car is in Excellent (maybe Concours), Good, Average or Poor condition or, perhaps, somewhere in between these categories.

Many enthusiasts' car magazines run a regular price guide. If you haven't bought the latest editions, do so now, and compare their suggested values for the model you are thinking of buying; also look at the auction prices they're reporting. The values published tend to vary from one magazine to another, as do their scales of condition, so read carefully the guidance notes they provide. Bear in mind that a recent show winner could be worth more than the highest scale published. Assuming that the car you have in mind is not in show/concours condition, then relate the level of condition that you judge the car to be in with the appropriate guide price. How does the figure compare with the asking price? Before you start haggling with the seller, consider what effect any variation from standard specification might have on the car's value. If you are buying from a dealer, remember there will be a dealer's premium on the price. Finally, values of the 16-valve models are climbing markedly, so don't wait too long!

Automatic transmission, air-conditioning and velour upholstery in this luxuriously-equipped 2.6.

Top marks for originality, if the car you are viewing still has a sought-after original Becker radio.

Desirable options/extras

Many of the features we now take for granted were expensive options when the 190 was launched; cars originally sold in Germany, in particular, often have a pretty basic 'spec,' with manual windows and cloth or vinyl (MB-Tex) seats. Even power steering originally cost extra: this makes a big difference to how the car drives and should be considered a 'must have.'

With all the cars at least 25 years' old, it makes sense to buy on condition and originality, rather than to hold out for rare options. Some commonly-found extras do, however, enhance the refined feel of the 'Baby Benz' – electric windows, a sunroof, leather upholstery and cruise control, for example. In the same way, many buyers prefer Mercedes' smooth automatic transmission, especially on the 2.6.

Air-conditioning was less often specified in Europe than the US, but is a welcome bonus. Mercedes' brochures often featured the 190 with luxurious velour upholstery, but this is an option rarely seen today.

Introduced in 1989, the Sportline trim package marked a new direction for Mercedes: the firmer suspension further improves the cars' excellent handling, while the optional bucket-style seats give better support when cornering. Both the 2.3-16 and 2.5-16 came with a specially developed five-speed manual gearbox: this suits their sporty feel, and many enthusiasts prefer it to the automatic.

Optional separate rear seats and check cloth trim on Sportline models.

Undesirable features

As the 190 emerges as a modern classic, originality becomes even more important. Countless aftermarket bodykits were offered when the 190 was new; some – from companies such as AMG, Duchatelet or Lorinser – were relatively well made, but many were not, and soon begin to look shabby. Many buyers will prefer the standard body to even the better-quality kits. Chrome wheelarch trims, more popular in the US than the UK, can also trap moisture and foster corrosion.

Many tuners – including Brabus, Carlsson and Oettinger – also offered performance upgrades for the 190. These were usually based on the four-cylinder petrol engine, although at least one firm squeezed a 5-litre V8 under the bonnet of the 190! If you don't mind a modified car, make sure that the conversion has been thoroughly engineered, with brakes and suspension uprated to match the increased performance.

Striking a deal

Negotiate on the basis of your condition assessment, mileage, and fault rectification cost. Also take into account the car's specification. Be realistic about the value, but don't be completely intractable: a small compromise on the part of the vendor or buyer will often facilitate a deal at little real cost.

Even well-made bodykits, such as those fitted to this 190E AMG first owned by Ringo Starr, will not appeal to all buyers.

13 Do you really want to restore?
– it'll take longer and cost more than you think

As with so many aspects of the 190, the answer to this question depends enormously on the model you are interested in. The extraordinary prices which the Evo and especially Evo II models currently fetch at auction or with high-end specialist dealers certainly make restoring them look an economic possibility. But then again, how many of these exotic models are likely to have been so neglected that they now need a full-scale restoration? And how certain would you be of finding all the parts unique to these models?

If, on the other hand, you are interested in one of the mainstream petrol or diesel-engined versions, it is currently hard to justify the cost of an extensive restoration. Although most routine service parts for the 190 are quite affordable, the price of replacement body parts soon adds up: a pair of front wings, for example, will cost nearly ●x1300, and that is before any prep work, fitting or painting. As one prominent US Mercedes specialist, Kent Bergsma, puts it: "There is nothing more expensive than a cheap Mercedes."

With nearly 1.9 million 190s sold new, and Mercedes-Benz' outstanding build quality, there are still a great many cars to choose from, especially for the most popular models like the 190E. Better, then, to continue looking, perhaps with the help of your local club, and extend your search to other parts of the country or neighbouring states. As well as cars which are already in excellent, original condition, you may come across a car which is mechanically and cosmetically sound, but just needs recommissioning after a period of inactivity (see Chapter 15 – Problems due to lack of use, for points to check on cars like these).

The 2.3-16 and 2.5-16 models have reached an interesting point in their history. Prices for original, low-mileage cars in excellent condition (especially with the sought-after manual transmission) are steadily increasing, to the point where a thorough overhaul or refurbishment could soon be justified. Take care to cost any such projects carefully, especially if specialist engine work is needed: all too often, one job leads to another, and another …

You may find some cars which have suffered accident damage and where the repairs would be too expensive for an insurance company to approve, but which can be purchased very cheaply and returned to roadworthy condition. Here again, it's unlikely that you will recoup your costs: potential buyers will always be apprehensive when you come to sell on cars like these. Be especially wary of the high-performance 16-valve cars, which may have suffered chassis damage as the result of a crash during a back-road blast or track day.

The costs of restoring a shabby or incomplete car soon mount up.
(Courtesy MTSV)

14 Paint problems

– bad complexion, including dimples, pimples and bubbles

The paint on the 190 was originally of high quality, pre-dating the problems with water-based paints which affected the W124 series after 1993. Paint faults generally occur due to lack of protection/maintenance, or to poor preparation prior to a respray or touch-up. Measuring the paint depth on each panel will help confirm if all the paint is original. Some of the following conditions may be present in the car you're looking at:

Orange peel

This appears as an uneven paint surface, similar to the skin of an orange. This fault is caused by the failure of atomized paint droplets to flow into each other when they hit the surface. It's sometimes possible to rub out the effect with proprietary paint cutting/rubbing compound or very fine grades of abrasive paper. A respray may be necessary in severe cases. Consult a bodywork repairer/paint shop for advice on the particular car.

Cracking

Severe cases are likely to have been caused by too heavy an application of paint (or filler beneath the paint). Also, insufficient stirring of the paint before application can lead to the components being improperly mixed, and cracking can result. Incompatibility with the paint already on the panel can have a similar effect. To rectify the problem, it is necessary to rub down to a smooth, sound finish before respraying the problem area.

Crazing

Sometimes the paint takes on a crazed rather than a cracked appearance when the problems mentioned under 'Cracking' are present. This problem can also be caused by a reaction between the underlying surface and the paint. Paint removal and respraying the problem area is usually the only solution.

Blistering

Almost always caused by corrosion of the metal beneath the paint. Usually perforation will be found in the metal and the damage will usually be worse than that suggested by the area of blistering. The metal will have to be repaired before repainting.

Micro blistering

Usually the result of an economy respray where inadequate heating has allowed moisture to settle on the car before spraying. Consult a paint specialist, but usually damaged paint will have to be removed before partial or full respraying. Can also be caused by car covers that don't 'breathe.'

Red paint can fade in strong sunlight. (Courtesy Mercedes-Benz Classic)

Fading
Some colours, especially reds, are prone to fading, if subjected to strong sunlight for long periods without the benefit of polish protection. Sometimes proprietary paint restorers and/or paint cutting/rubbing compounds will retrieve the situation. Often a respray is the only real solution.

Peeling
Often a problem with metallic paintwork when the sealing lacquer becomes damaged and begins to peel off. Poorly applied paint may also peel. The remedy is to strip and start again!

Dimples
Dimples in the paintwork are caused by the residue of polish (particularly silicone types) not being removed properly before respraying. Paint removal and repainting is the only solution.

Dents
Small dents are usually easily cured by the 'Dentmaster' or equivalent process, that sucks or pushes out the dent (as long as the paint surface is still intact). Companies offering dent removal services usually come to your home: consult your telephone directory or search online.

www.velocebooks.com / www.veloce.co.uk
Details of all current books • New book news • Special offers • Gift vouchers • Forum

53

15 Problems due to lack of use

– just like their owners, 190s need exercise!

The 190 is one of Mercedes' most durable models, and will soak up the miles without complaint. Lack of use, on the other hand, can cause problems.

Seized and rusted components

Pistons in callipers, slave and master cylinders can seize. The parking brake can also seize if the cables and linkages rust, particularly on cars with automatic transmission, whose owners may not use it at all, simply putting the transmission selector in 'P.'

Fluids

All filters and fluids should be replaced at regular intervals, and, if fitted, the air-conditioning recharged. Good-quality coolant is essential to avoid premature corrosion of the aluminium components in the engine, cooling and heating system, and to avoid the risk of serious damage. Silt settling and solidifying can result in overheating.

Brake fluid absorbs water from the atmosphere and should be renewed every two years.

Fuel system

On cars which are not used regularly, the fuel-injection system can play up: the O-rings around the injector nozzles become brittle and cause air leaks, in turn resulting in jerky acceleration. On the original 190 model, the carburettor needle can stick.

Tyre problems

Tyres that have had the weight of the car on them in a single position for some time will develop flat spots, resulting in some (usually temporary) vibration. The tyre walls may have cracks or (blister-type) bulges, meaning new tyres are needed. Even if the tyres appear to be in good condition, check the DOT code on the sidewall, which will show the week and year of manufacture.

Even though this car has covered less than 30,000 miles, the bulkhead insulation foam has completely perished.

Shock absorbers (dampers)
With lack of use, the dampers will lose their elasticity or even seize. Creaking, groaning and stiff suspension are signs of this problem.

Rubber and plastic
Radiator hoses may have perished and split, possibly resulting in the loss of all coolant. Window, door and rear light seals can all harden and leak. Gaiters and boots can crack. Wiper blades will harden. The insulation foam under the bonnet will perish.

Interior trim
On cars fitted with leather upholstery, the hide needs regular conditioning (every six months) if it is to stay supple. Cars left in the sun can suffer from dried or cracked dashboards. Velour or cloth trim can fade, especially in exposed areas, such as the top of the rear seat.

Electrics
The battery will be of little use if it has not been charged for many months. If a car is left standing for several weeks, connecting it to a trickle charger will keep it in good condition. If acid has been allowed to leak out from the battery, the tray underneath it may have rusted through.

Earthing/grounding problems are common when the connections have corroded. Wiring insulation can harden and fail. The electric windows can seize, particularly in the rear, where they are used less frequently. The speedometer cable can dry out, resulting in the needle fluttering.

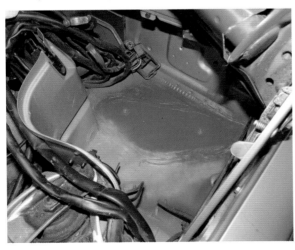

The battery tray on this car had rusted through completely, and new metal has been let in. (Courtesy MTSV)

Rotting exhaust system
Exhaust gas contains a high water content, so exhaust systems corrode very quickly from the inside, when the car is not used. This even applies to stainless steel systems.

16 The community

– key people, organisations and companies in the 190 world

Owners of the 190 will find plenty of organisations and individuals ready to help them look after their cars.

Clubs

Mercedes-Benz lends its support to more than 80 independent clubs worldwide, and many of these have model registers dedicated to the 190 (often referred to by enthusiasts as the W201, its internal designation). Benefits available to members include technical helplines and other information, discounted services such as insurance, professionally produced club magazines and the chance to join frequent social and driving events. You can find out more at:
• Mercedes-Benz Classic (factory homepage): mercedes-benz.com/en/mercedes-benz/classic/classic-overview/
• UK: mercedes-benz-club.co.uk
• North America: mbca.org
• Other countries: specials.mercedes-benz-classic.com/en/club/#ger/

Silver 190E 2.5-16 and blue 190E 2.3 at an enthusiasts' meeting in France.

Specialists

In North America, it's worth starting with one of the 85 local sections of the club, which should be able to recommend a dealer or workshop near you.

In the UK, one company has made the 190 its speciality: MTSV, based in West Yorkshire (mtsv.co.uk). Merparts in Inverclyde (merparts.com) is also a top 190 specialist, with particular expertise in looking after the 16-valve models.

Many other independent Mercedes specialists such as these often sell 190s, and can handle servicing and other repair work on them:
• Cheshire Classic Benz: ccbenz.co.uk
• Edward Hall (Buckinghamshire): edward-hall.co.uk
• John Haynes Mercedes (West Sussex): john-haynes.com
• Steve Redfearn Motor Co (London): call 020 8540 2311

You will find listings for many other companies in the club directories and in the magazines below.

Parts and accessories

Many service parts remain available from your local Mercedes-Benz dealer, with support from the factory in Germany, or the Mercedes-Benz Classic Center in Irvine, California. Their prices can sometimes be high, so you may prefer to order online from an independent parts supplier such as these:
• UK – Mercedes Parts Centre: mercedes-parts-centre.co.uk
• UK – PFS Parts: partsformercedes-benz.com
• US – Pelican Parts: pelicanparts.com/catalog/

Useful sources of information

Three English-language magazines cater to classic Mercedes enthusiasts and often feature the 190:
• *Mercedes Enthusiast* (monthly – mercedesenthusiast.co.uk)
• *Classic Mercedes* (quarterly – classicmercedesmagazine.com)
can both be found at large newsstands in both the UK and North America, or obtained on subscription
• *Mercedes-Benz Classic* is published in English and German by Mercedes itself three times a year: subscribe at mercedes-benz.com/en/mercedes-benz/lifestyle/mercedes-benz-magazines/classic-magazine/subscription/

At the time of writing, there is no English-language book exclusively dedicated to the 190. Brooklands Books (brooklandsbooks.co.uk), however, devotes one of its excellent compilations of period road tests to the 190: *Mercedes 190 Limited Edition Extra 1983-1993*.

For enthusiasts who want to carry out repair work themselves, Kent Bergsma's informative Mercedessource channel on YouTube features more than 60 'How-To' videos on the 190. Haynes also covers the 190 in its series of *Workshop Manuals*. In the UK, the official club (mercedes-benz-club.co.uk) has archived a large number of very helpful features from its magazine, covering common problems and how to repair them. Even if you do not plan on doing the work yourself, these resources provide valuable guidance on how difficult (and potentially expensive) a job may be.

17 Vital statistics
– essential data at your fingertips

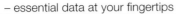

Production figures

Model	Production period	Number of units
190	1982-1991	118,561
190E 1.8	1990-1993	173,354
190E/ 190E 2.0	1982-1993	638,180
190E 2.3	1983-1993	186,610
190E 2.6	1986-1993	104,907*
190E 2.3-16	1984-1988	19,487
190E 2.5-16	1988-1993	5743
190E 2.5-16 Evolution	1989	502
190E 2.5-16 Evolution II	1990	502
190D	1983-1993	452,806
190D 2.2	1983-1985	10,560
190D 2.5	1985-1993	147,502
190D 2.5 Turbo	1986-1993	20,915
Total		1,879,629

* Includes 190E 3.2 AMG.

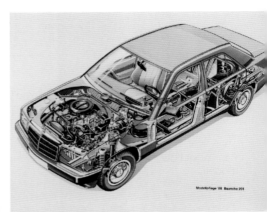

Cutaway view of the face-lifted 190 from 1988. (Courtesy Mercedes-Benz Classic)

Technical specifications
Petrol models

Model	Engine capacity (cc)	Engine type	Configuration	Peak power (bhp) at rpm	Maximum torque (lb-ft) at rpm	Transmissions available
190 (1982-1984)	1997	M102	4cyl in-line, 8V	90/5000	122/2500	4M/5M or 4A
190 (1984-1988)	1997	M102	4cyl in-line, 8V	105/5200	125/2500	4M/5M or 4A
190E 1.8	1797	M102	4cyl in-line, 8V	109/5500	111/3700	4M/5M or 4A
190E/190E 2.0	1997	M102	4cyl in-line, 8V	122/5100	131/3500	4M/5M or 4A
190E 2.3	2299/2298 (from 1991)	M102	4cyl in-line, 8V	136/5100	151/3500	5M or 4A
190E 2.6	2597	M103	6cyl in-line, 12V	166/5800	168/4600	5M or 4A
190E 2.3-16	2299	M102	4cyl in-line, 16V	185/6200	173/4500	5M or 4A
190E 2.5-16	2498	M102	4cyl in-line, 16V	204/6750	177/5000-5500	5M or 4A
190E 2.5-16 Evolution	2463	M102	4cyl in-line, 16V	204/6750	177/5000-550	5M
190E 2.5-16 Evolution II	2463	M102	4cyl in-line, 16V	235/7200	181/5000-6000	5M

Note: with the exception of the Evo II, all figures shown are for cars *without* catalytic converters, which slightly reduced power.

Diesel models

Model	Engine capacity (cc)	Engine type	Configuration	Peak power (bhp) at rpm	Maximum torque (lb-ft) at rpm	Transmissions available
190D	1997	OM601	4cyl in-line	72/4600	91/2800	4M/5M or 4A
190D 2.2	2197	OM601	4cyl in-line	73/4200	96/2800	5M or 4A
190D 2.5	2497	OM602	5cyl in-line	90/4600	114/2800	5M or 4A
190D 2.5 Turbo	2497	OM602	5cyl in-line	122/4600	166/2400	4A or 5M (from 1989)

Running gear

Independent suspension all round, with multi-link rear suspension, front and rear anti-roll bars, anti-dive and anti-squat geometry. Hydropneumatic self-levelling rear suspension on 2.3-16 and 2.5-16 models.
Steering by recirculating ball, with power assistance standard on all models from 1985.
Four-wheel disc brakes, with ABS optional and then standard (date varies by model).
14in or 15in wheels in 1983/84, depending on model, then 15in on all models.

Performance figures: selected models

Model	Top speed	Acceleration: 0-100kph (62mph) in seconds
190 manual (1982-1984)	109mph (175kph)	13.2
190E 1.8 manual	115mph (185kph)	12.3
190E 2.0 automatic	118mph (190kph)	10.5
190E 2.3 automatic	121mph (195kph)	10.3
190E 2.6 automatic	130mph (210kph)	8.9
190E 2.3-16 manual	143mph (230kph)	7.5
190E 2.5-16 manual	146mph (235kph)	7.5
190D manual	99mph (160kph)	18.1
190D 2.5 manual	108mph (174kph)	14.8
190D 2.5 Turbo automatic	119mph (192kph)	11.5

Note: all figures shown are for cars *without* catalytic converters.
Source: Marco Ruiz, *Mercedes-Benz 1991-2001* (Opera Omnia).

Dimensions

Model	190D/E until 1988	190D/E from 1988	190E 2.3-16/2.5-16
Length	174.0in/4420mm	175.1in/4448mm	174.4in/4430mm
Width	66.1in/1678mm	66.5in/1690mm	67.2in/1706mm
Height	54.7in/1390mm	54.7in/1390mm	53.6in/1361mm
Wheelbase	104.9in/2665mm	104.9in/2665mm	104.9in/2665mm
Fuel tank	14.5US gal/55l	14.5US gal/55l	18.5US gal/70l
Luggage capacity	14.5ft3/410l	14.5ft3/410l	13.6ft3/385l
Weight	2381-2756lb/ 1080-1250kg	2557-2866lb/ 1160-1300kg	2777-2866lb/ 1260-1300kg

The Essential Buyer's Guide™ series ...

... don't buy a vehicle until you've read one of these!

Also from Veloce Publishing –

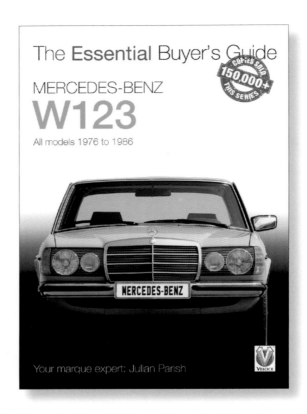

Looking for the perfect blend of classic Mercedes style and everyday usability? Available as a saloon/sedan, estate/wagon or coupé, the W123 can make a great choice, if you know what to look out for. Follow the helpful guidance in this book to assess a promising car like a professional, and find the right car at the right price!

ISBN: 978-1-845849-26-9
Paperback • 19.5x13.9cm • 64 pages • 102 pictures

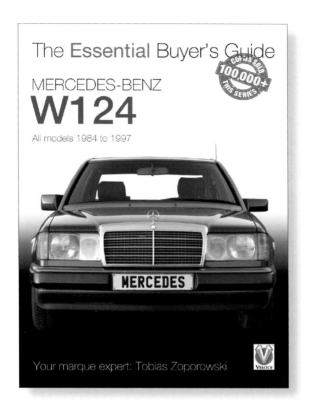

The Essential Buyer's Guide

MERCEDES-BENZ
W124

All models 1984 to 1997

100,000+ COPIES SOLD THIS SERIES

Your marque expert: Tobias Zoporowski

VELOCE

Having this book in your pocket is just like having a real marque expert by your side. Benefit from the author's years of Mercedes-Benz ownership, learn how to spot a bad car quickly, and how to assess a promising car like a professional. Get the right car at the right price!

ISBN: 978-1-845848-77-4
Paperback • 19.5x13.9cm • 64 pages • 100 pictures

Index